ACHIEVEMENT MOTIVATION

DR. SAVITA MISHRA

Contents

Preface

Achievement Motivation is the attitude to achieve rather than the achievements themselves. It can be considered as extended person-intrinsic motivation because its reinforcement is delayed. It arises from an interaction within the person. Achievement motivation is a pattern of planning of actions and of feelings connected with striving to achieve some internalized standard of excellence, as contrasted for example, will power or friendship.

Need for achievement can be defined as a motive to strive for success. Parents who demand that their children do things on their own at an early age, and do them well are likely to instill the need for achievement. A second factor concerns the use of rewards and punishments by parents. It appears that independence training combined with rewards and affection for behaving independently are responsible for instilling the need for achievement in young boys. Thus it can be concluded that individuals with high need for achievement are people interested in excellence for its own sake rather than for the extrinsic rewards. If their personal responsibility affects the outcome, they tend to prefer to control their destinies and make independent judgements based on their own evaluations and experience. They choose challenging goals and prefer delayed larger rewards to immediate smaller rewards.

Dr. Savita Mishra

CHAPTER ONE

ACHIEVEMENT MOTIVATION

Academic achievement is of paramount importance, particularly in the present Socio- economic and Cultural contexts. Obviously, in the school great emphasis is placed on achievement right from the beginning of formal education. The school has its own systematic hierarchy which is largely based on achievement and performance rather than ascription or quality.

The effectiveness of any educational system is gauged to the extent the pupils involved in the system achieve, whether it be in Cognitive, Affective or Psychomotor domain. In general terms, achievement refers to the scholastic or academic achievement of the student at the end of an educational programme. Academic performance being globally viewed as a most important factor for students for pursuing higher education.

For Academic performance many factors are responsible which are independent in character, those are called the correlates of achievement. Correlates of achievement are viewed in terms of three domains. These are Cognitive, Affective and Psychomotor as described below:

- *The cognitive factor relates to 'intellectual capacity' of learner like intelligence, aptitude, creativity etc;*
- *The affective factor relates to the feeling of interest, attitude, adjustment etc; and*
- *The psychomotor aspect relates to skills, manipulation etc.*

In addition to the innate mental abilities, very recently, the non-scholastic factor's contribution towards Academic Achievement has been highlighted in context of total personal development of a child because having endowed with highest amount of primary and intellectual ability, if the student does not culture a habit in respect of seriousness in achieving the conquest, he can not show excellence in the field of academics. He must have proper study habits, needs for achievement, highest level of aspiration, a good mental health, proper adjustment, interest towards studies etc. for academic excellence. Therefore, these factors of non-scholastic character play major role in the field of academic achievement.

According to *Maslow (1954),* the need for achievement is an important factor for cognitive performance. This is known as achievement motivation.

1.1 Achievement Motivation

A school child exhibits a number of concerns like making and retaining friendship with other boys and girls, setting the reward and approval of teachers and parents, desiring to become monitor of the class. Concerns of the boys such as these are indicative of motives. The desire to improve performance at school or to get a good grade is indicative of achievement motive. Achievement motive and behavior as a component of academic achievement has been the matter of research in the recent years. The investigations conducted by *Ghuman (1976),Tripathy (1986)* and *Singh (1986)* throw highlight to this. The concept therefore needs elaboration.

In the area of achievement motivation, the work on goal-theory has differentiated three separate types of goals : Mastery goals (also called learning goals) which focus on gaining competence or mastering a new set of knowledge or skills; Performance goals (also called ego-involvement goals) which focus on achieving normative- based standards, doing better than others, or doing well without a lot of effort; and Social goals which focus on relationships among people *(Ames, 1992; Dweck, 1986, Urdan & Maehr, 1995).* In the context of school learning, which involves operating in a relatively structured environment; students with mastery goals outperform students with either performance or social goals. However, in life success, it seems critical that individuals have all three types of goals in order to be very successful.

1.2.Meaning of Achievement Motivation

Achievement Motivation is the attitude to achieve rather than the achievements themselves. It can be considered as extended person-intrinsic motivation because its reinforcement is delayed. It arises from an interaction within the person. Achievement motivation is *"a pattern of planning of actions and of feelings connected with striving to achieve some internalized standard of excellence, as contrasted for example, will power or friendship" (Vidler, 1977).*

Need for achievement can be defined as a motive to strive for success. Early attempt by *McClelland (1950)* was made to find out how need for achievement is reflected in societies and how as a societal value it affects the economic and political growth of a nation. He measured the need for achievement with Thematic Apperception Test (T.A.T.) after McClelland his colleagues devised their method of measuring need for achievement. They attempted to find out how those who were low and those who were high in this motive differed. Parents who demand that their children do things on their own at an early age, and do them well are likely to instill the need for achievement (*McClelland, 1953; Writer bottom, 1958*). A second factor concerns the use of rewards and punishments by parents. It appears that independence training combined with rewards and affection for behaving independently are responsible for instilling the need for achievement in young boys. (**Teevan and Mc,Ghee, 1972**). Thus it can be concluded that individuals with high need for achievement are people interested in excellence for its own sake rather than for the extrinsic rewards. If their personal responsibility affects the outcome, they tend to prefer to control their destinies and make independent judgements based on their own evaluations and experience. They choose challenging goals and prefer delayed larger rewards to immediate smaller rewards.

Understanding the factors that affect achievement is important because motivation affects achievement and level of occupation (*Farmer, 1985*).*Murray* (1938) described achievement motivation as the desire to "*accomplish something difficult...to overcome obstacles and attain a high standard; to excel oneself*". *Burger (1997)* indicated that high-need achievers are moderate risk takers, have an energetic approach to work, and prefer jobs that give them personal responsibility for outcomes. *McClelland and Pilon (1983)* proposed that parents promoted the need for achievement by providing support and encouragement. However, as *Burger (1997)* indicated, it is important that parents provide enough support to allow the child to develop a sense of personal competence without robbing the child of independence and initiative.

That is, parents must reward their children's accomplishment, but too much involvement might leave the child with an undermined sense of accomplishment. Parental level of education influences parental involvement and parental support of and educational expectations for their children. In turn, parental involvement and support and expectations for their children influence the adolescents' achievement motivation. School climate is expected to influence teacher expectations for and support of their students. Finally, it is hypothesized that the school climate and teacher expectations have a direct relationship with achievement motivation as described in Figure 1 below:

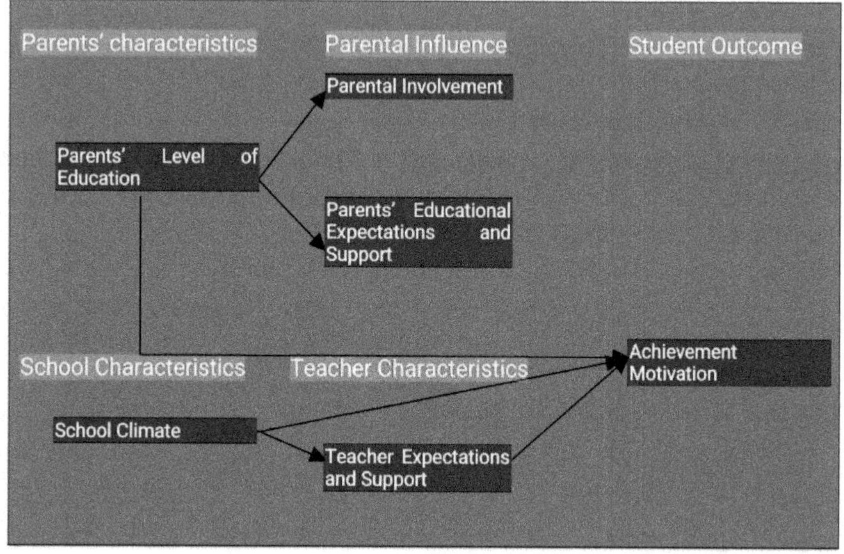

Figure 1.Hypothesized model of influences on adolescents' achievement motivation

The achievement motive is being studied both in relation to economic growth and in academic performance, *McClelland (1961,1953),Atkinson (1958).* These studies highlight the importance of the formation of the standard of excellence in the development of proper study motivation in children. *Kagan and Howord (1962)* have summarized researches showing the importance of mastery behavior in the general development of the child and his personality. *Flanagan (1964)* has pointed out that the basic motivating factors leading man to work long hours under unsatisfactory conditions are not related to good working conditions. These factors are likely to be most effective motivators of studies.

Previous reviews by *Rao, Mehta and Rao (1979)* indicate growing interest in achievement motivation research covering the period 1967-75. The research has primarily concentrated on the antecedents of n-ach, n-ach; and achievement relationships, development of n-ach measures, and motivation training. The intervention studies to enhance n-ach. among school children are a remarkable feature of research on the Indian scene.

As the authors stated, *"viewed broadly, researchers on motivation in general and achievement motivation in particular seem to be developing fast, touching many new areas"*. Studies reported during the period under review also take three different directions: assessment of n-ach; correlates of n-ach. and effects of n-ach. on achievement.

Anand and Dave (1979) reviewed the literature on correlates of achievement over 1972-78. The trend report was organized according to general correlates, SES, Personality, curriculum organization and over and under achievement, intelligence, n-ach., parental encouragement, emotional climate and educational facilities in the home was related to academic achievement. Most of the studies on SES and academic achievement are replications or repetitions, establishing the same functional relationship between SEs and achievement as earlier reported in the survey of Research in Educational Psychology *(Buch, 1972)*. Personality studies identified certain values, motives and non-cognitive traits influencing achievement while n-ach. was found to be a pre-requisites to high academic achievement, *{Mukherjee (1969); Sharma (1979); Patel (1981); Mohanty (1998); and Nayak (2004)}*.

Achievement motivation is a complex area in terms of concept and measurements However, the studies mentioned above attempted quite reliably to measure its nature, correlates and effects on behaviour. Studies relating to training for enhancing achievement motivation are very rare *(Raghava, 1985)*. It has been firmly established by now that academic achievement is affected by personality variables, curricular variable, and societal variables and so on. Sufficient data are available on the relationship of many of these variables with achievement. It may be noticed that SES, which is a composite of sub-variables like parents' income, father's educational level, mother's educational level, educational facilities available at home, etc. has been found to fluctuate under different conditions in its relationship with achievement at school.

1.3.Effects of Achievement Motivation on Behaviour

The need for achievement appears to have a significant effect upon one's life. Compared with those who have low levels of this motive, individuals with high levels are likely to do better in college, are more apt to be business people than professionals, and are more likely to become enterpreneurs. It was demonstrated that under some circumstances high need for achievement people will persist longer at a challenging task. Challenge, especially that of marks or grades in school, has been investigated but since need for achievement is considered to be an intrinsic motivator and independent of external reinforcers such as grades and prizes, it cannot be expected that there should be a high correlation between it and school achievement. Yet a number of studies have found some support for this position *(McClelland, 1958).* Since need for achievement is regarded as a learned motivation, training programmes have been developed for children to enhance their levels of it, and encouraging findings have demonstrated that even though academic grades may not have improved greatly, purposeful planning and action in many phases of life have resulted. While people in our society may value achievement motivation, the drive to be successful is not without liabilities. It means long hours at work that take away time from family and friends.

Therefore, the need for achievement appears to have a significant effect upon the correlates of academic achievement. The individual assesses his or her behaviour through achievement motivation because the need for achievement centres round the attitude to achievement rather than the achievements. Both n-ach. and anxiety are acquired primarily on the basis of learning and experience. And the need to achieve success is thought to be acquired through the inherent biological factors in case of human being. In the present investigation the need for achievement is considered in terms of its impact on academic achievement.

In general, explanations regarding the sources of motivation can be categorized as either extrinsic (outside the person) or intrinsic (internal to the person). Intrinsic sources and corresponding theories can be further subcategories as either body/ physical, mind, mental or transpersonal / spiritual as illustrated in figure – 2 below:

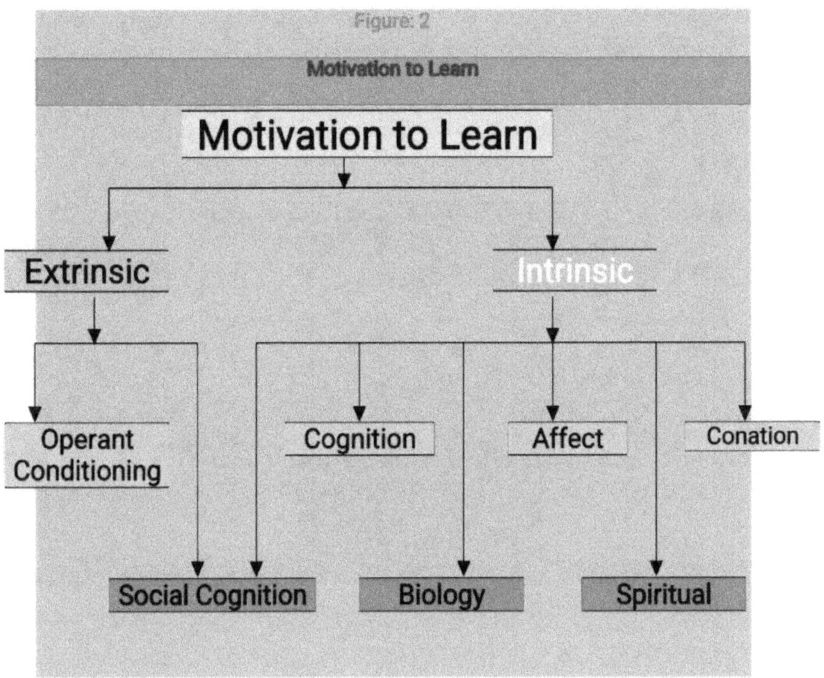

The environment, an individual's behavior and the individual's characteristics (*e.g. knowledge. emotion, cognitive development*) both influence and are influenced by each other two components as shown in Figure – 3 below:

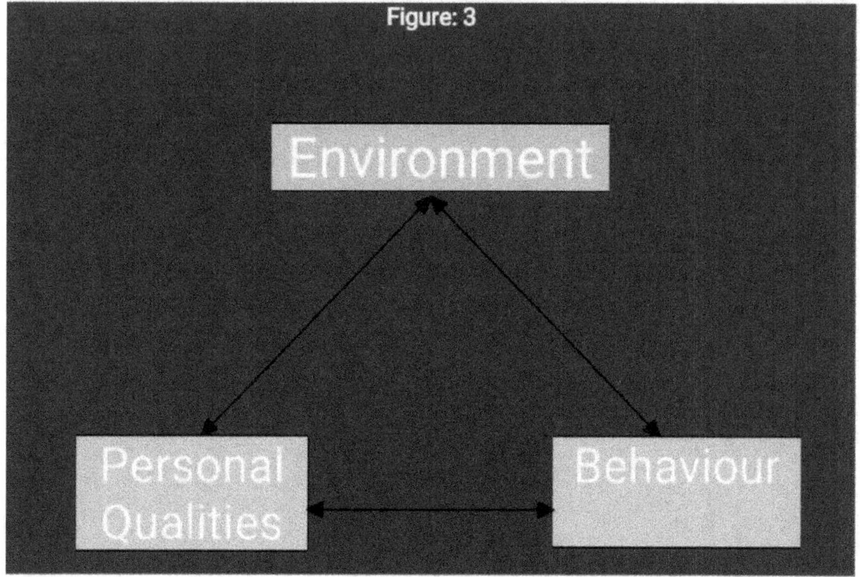

1.4Achievement Motivation and Academic performance

McClelland (1961) has provided ample evidence in support of the achievement motivation and economic growth. He has argued and proposed that societies having high n' achievement show greater economic growth than those low in n' achievement. Empirical evidence on the relationship of n' achievement and academic performance has been inadequate. ***Riccuiti et al (1955)*** found out a positive correlation (0.23 to 0.33) between n-achievement and school grades.

McClelland (1953) reported inconclusive evidence on the relationship between n-achievement and school performance. ***Unlinger and Stephens(1960)*** found relationship between n' achievement and school grades in case of students of superior ability only. Therefore, it may be concluded that there exists some kind of relationship between the level of achievement motivation and academic achievement.

1.5Studies showing relationship between Achievement Motivation and Academic Achievement

Research studies in academic achievement have been a recent phenomenon. All the researches have been primarily concentrated on the antecedent: of n-ach. n-ach and achievement relationship, development of n-ach measures and motivation training.

Ghuman (1976) conducted a study of aptitudes, personality traits and achievement motivation of academic over achievers and under achievers. The sample of the study consisted of 1,948 students of both sexes, studying in grades IX, X and XI of the various higher secondary schools of Raipur district of Madhya Pradesh opting for different academic streams. The major findings of the study were:

i. *The over achievers and under achievers did not differ significantly on any of the independent variables, namely, aptitudes, achievement motivation or personality traits.*

ii. *The over-achievers, regardless of sex possessed high achievement motivation whereas the under achievers possessed relatively low achievement motivation.*

Abrol (1977) studied achievement motivation in relation to intelligence, vocational interests, achievement, sex and socio-economic status (SES), with a sample of 414 students of class X from six higher secondary schools from the urban area of Delhi. The mean n-ach scores of boys were significantly greater than that of girls. A significant and positive correlation of moderate value was found between achievement motivation and scholastic achievement.

Ghuman (1978) studied achievement motivation of over achievers and under-achievers with a sample of 1,948 students of both sexes studying in grade IX, X and XI of the various higher secondary schools of Raipur district of Madhya Pradesh opting for different stream namely humanities, science and commerce. It was found that the over- achievers and under-achievers did not differ significantly on achievement motivation, the over-achievers, regardless of sex possessed high achievement motivation whereas the under-achievers possessed relatively low achievement motivation.

Gupta (1978) studied anxiety and achievement motivation in relation to academic achievement, sex and economic status with a sample 360 students (180 boys and 180 girls) randomly drawn from classes IX & X. Boys were found to possess more achievement motivation than girls.

Hussain (1979) studied recall of finished and interrupted tasks (I/T) under ego and task oriented conditions in relation to anxiety, need achievement and need for approval motive as personality variables. *The* *major findings were:*

i. *High anxiety (HA) group differed significantly from the low anxiety (LA) group under ego-oriented conditions. The LA group recalled I/T better while HA group preferred completed tasks.*

ii. *Both the HA and the LA groups differed significantly in their recall of C/I under task oriented conditions. The LA group recalled C/T tasks better while the HA group recalled I/T better.*

iii. *The low n- achievement group in the recall of C/I tasks under ego oriented conditions differed significantly from high n-achievement group. The low n-achievement group recalled C/T better while Hn-Ach group recalled I/T better.*

iv. *Both the Hb- achievement and the low n' ach groups differed significantly in their recall of C/I tasks under task oriented conditions. The low n-ach group recalled I/T better which the high n-ach group recalled C/T better. (I/T is interrupted task, C/I is complete interrupted task and C/T is complete task)*

Narula (1979) in a study of achievement motivation, personal preferences, perception, anxiety, risk taking behaviour and other co-relates in relation to intelligence, socio-economic status and performance of the prospective secondary school teachers of Orissa found out that the males scored more than females on measures of n-ach.

Jerath (1979) in a study of achievement motivation and its personality motivation and ability correlates found that:

i. *Males scores higher than the females on fantasy measures, n achievement, intelligence test, factors B, C, E, H of the 16 PF, theoretical, economic and political interests.*

ii. *Females scored higher than males on factors A.I.O.Q3 and Q4 of 16 PF, aesthetic, social and religious interest.*

iii. *Factor analysis yielded the following comparable factors among males and females: anxiety, introversion Vs. Extraversion, body measures, scholastic proficiency and good upbringing.*

iv. *Four separate factors named 'Pathemia Vs. Cortertia' and 'Secure Naturalness Vs. Foxiness' were located in the male samples whereas in the female samples separate factors located were n-achievement and intelligence.*

v. *Among females n-ach and self sentiment could not be adequate matched with the factors obtained for the male samples.*

vi. *N-ach emerged as the complex measure in both males and females but with loadings entirely different factors.*

In the study of the effect of the achievement motivation in academic success with a sample of 450 students drawn randonmly from various colleges in the city of Ahmedebad, Siddique (1979) found that n-ach differed significantly in the urban and rural pupils.

Zargar (1980) in a study of expression, neuroticism and n-achievement in relation to intelligence, creativity and scholastic achievement found that the high need achievers had a high degree of creativity (verbal) whereas low need achievers had a high degree of non-verbal creativity. And the high need achievers had a better scholastic achievement than the low need achievers.

Shivappa (1980) took n-ach as one of the factors affecting academic achievement of high school pupils and his study was confined to 900 class X pupil (510 Boys and 390 girls) of selected high schools of North Bangalore. The major findings f the study that the study habits, educational aspirations and n-ach were significant positive co-relates of academic achievement.

Vats (1980) conducted a study on biochemical correlates of scholastic achievement, achievement motivation, creative functioning and anxiety. The sample consists of 150 male students and the findings of the study were:

i. *Biochemical substances did not show significant relationship with scholastic achievement;*

ii. *Varimax rotated factor analysis yielded 9 factors: Non-verbal creativity, verbal creativity, n–ach accomplishment, physical factor, physio-chemical factor, bio-chemical factor, stress anxiety and maturity.*

Sheel (1981) studied task performance as a function of n-achievement, anxiety and creativity among male and female adolescents. He found that:

i. *Need achievement had an important and significant positive relationship to task performance among both male and female adolescent. It was the high need achievement which favoured task performance.*

ii. *Need achievement conditions relaxed (R), neutral (N) and aroused (A) were found to task performance patterns like RNA. This pattern was common at high and low level of fluency, flexibility and originality as well as at high and low levels of anxiety.*
iii. *Task performance of male student having very high- high level of n-achievement and test anxiety was better than students of high-low, low-low and low-high level of n-achievement and test anxiety. Similarly, student having low high level had better performance than low-low and high-low of n-achievement and test anxiety.*

Singh (1981) in a study of anxiety and the need achievement in relation tester's set found that the subjects having high need achievement scores showed higher expectancy effect than those having low and achievement scores.

Prakash (1981) conducted an experimental study of achievement motivation with a sample of 324 class IX boys and girls in Meerut and found that the performance in a linear programme on Hindi vocabulary building of high achievement motivation group has higher than that of an average and low achievement motivation groups, the average achievement motivation subjects had higher achievement than the low achievement motivation subjects.

Rajeeva (1982) in a study of achievements motive its correlates and performance of IX grade pupils of secondary schools of Bangalore found that:

i. *There was significant difference between classroom trust scores of high and low achievement motivated students;*
ii. *There was significant difference between the perception scores of high and low achievement motivated student;*
iii. *There was significant difference between the anxiety score of high and low achievement motivated students;*
iv. *There was significant difference between the achievement scores of high and low achievement motivated students.*

Gandhi (1982) investigated the relationship of academic achievement with achievement motivation with a sample of 339 boys and 448 girls. It was found that there was no significant sex difference with respect to achievement motive, achievement motive was significantly and positively related to academic achievement of high school student of both the sexes; the academic achievement of high school boys and girls was significantly affected by their scores as high average and low levels of achievement motive.

Chatterji (1983) took a project on comparative study of personality, intelligence and achievement motivation of students in different academic groups. One of the most important objectives was to compare the personality, intelligence and achievement motivation of successful and unsuccessful students at +2 stages. The major findings were:

i. *Scores on achievement motivation of students of science or commerce were significantly higher than others;*
ii. *Science students were significantly higher in achievement motivation in comparison with the arts and the agriculture groups;*
iii. *Scores on intelligence test in science group were significantly higher than that of all other academic groups with respect to all factors of intelligence viz., verbal, numerical and reasoning.*

Gupta (1983) in a study of personality characteristics of IXth grade over and under achieving boys and girls at different levels of achievement motivation found that:

i. *The group of low motivated over-achieving boys was found to be more vigorous and zestful than the group of low motivated under achieving boys. Among the under achieving boys, the low motivated group was found to be least vigorous and zestful;*
ii. *The high motivated under achieving girls were more submissive and less tense than high motivated over achieving girls. But low motivated under achieving girls were less submissive and more tensed than the low motivated over achieving girls;*
iii. *The average motivated boys did not differ from low motivated boys in scholastic ability;*
iv. *There was significant interaction in academic achievement and achievement motivation both in the case of boys as well as girls in the case of personality factor.*

Jain (1983) conducted a study on concept formation as a function on verbal intelligence and achievement motivation. He found that achievement motivation had a significant affect upon the concept formation ability of the students and highly motivated pupils showed a significantly superior ability in concept formation to those of low motivated pupils. The study also revealed that there existed positive linear significant relationship between the students' scores on the test of concept formation and verbal intelligence as well as their scores on concept formation and achievement motivation.

Chauhan (1984) made a comparative study of achievement motivation of schedules tribe and scheduled caste students of Himachal Pradesh in relation to their intelligence and Socio- economic status. The main findings of the study were:

i. *Scheduled Tribe and Scheduled Caste students did not differ significantly in relation to their achievement motivation. However Scheduled caste boys and girls had slightly higher achievement motivation than the Scheduled tribe boys and girls;*

ii. *Boys and girls did not differ significantly in relation to their achievement motivation;*

iii. *Community and Sex did not interact significantly in relation to the achievement motivation of students;*

iv. *The achievement motivation of students differ significantly at different levels of intelligence: high, middle and low;*

v. *Community and intelligence did not interact significantly in relation to achievement motivation of students;*

vi. *Sex and intelligence did not interact significantly in relation to the achievement motivation of students;*

vii. *Community, sex and intelligence did not interact significantly in relation to the achievement motivation of students.*

Ahluwalia (1985) in a study of factors affecting achievement motivation found that:

i. *Sex of the child had no effect on achievement motivation;*

ii. *Age was significantly and positively related to achievement motivation;*

iii. *Achievement motivation was not affected by birth order;*

iv. *Academic performance was positively and significantly related with achievement motivation;*

v. *Father's education significantly affected achievement motivation while mother's education had no effect on the achievement motivation of children;*

vi. *The achievement motivation was not affected either by father's occupation or mother's occupation;*

vii. *Economic status of parents did not affect achievement motivation;*

viii. *Urban/ Rural upbringing of children had no effect on achievement motivation of children;*

ix. *Size of family did not show any significant relationship with achievement motivation;*

x. *Dependency and achievement motivation were found to be negatively related though not significantly;*

xi. *Children of co-educational schools had more achievement motivation than children of boy's school. But no significant influence was recorded in the children of co-educational schools and girls schools, these of boys schools and girls schools;*

xii. *Children from Central schools were most achievement motivated next in order were Public schools followed by Government schools;*

xiii. *The organisational climate in different types of schools did not significantly affect the achievement motivation of children.*

From the above review of researches the evidences in support of the hypothesis that n' achievement is related to academic achievement are prominent. In the above backdrop, the present study endeavours to examine the relationship of n' achievement and academic performance.

1.6. Rationale of the study

The world is becoming more and more competitive. Quality of performance has become the key factor for personal progress. Parents desire that their children climb the ladder of performance to as high a level as possible. This desire for a high level of achievement puts a lot of pressure on students, teachers, schools and in general, the educational system itself. In fact, it appears as if the whole system of education revolves around the academic achievement of students, though various other outcomes are also expected from the system. Thus, a lot of time and effort of the schools are used for helping students to achieve better in their scholastic endeavours.

It is perceived that there is strong relationship between the academic performance of school children and their motivation level to achieve excellence in education. This study is an effort to ascertain the extent to which achievement motivation of secondary school children of different sex groups and different socio-economic strata, affect their academic performance.

CHAPTER TWO

STATEMENT OF THE PROBLEM

This study is undertaken with a view to find solutions to the following problems in relation to achievement motivation of the students:

- The variations of Achievement Motivation of students of secondary school in relation to gender and socio - economic status;

- Difference in the Academic Achievement of secondary school children in relation to gender and socio economic status variations;

- Difference between Academic Achievement and Achievement Motivation of secondary school children due to gender and socio economic status variations;

- Degree of relationship between Achievement Motivation and Academic Achievement of secondary school children with regard to gender and socio - economic status variations;

- Extent of contribution of Achievement Motivation to Academic Achievement in relation to gender and socio - economic status variations.

2.1.Objectives of the study
The objectives of the study are:

- To ascertain achievement motivation of the students of secondary schools in relation to gender and socio- economic status variations;

- To determine the academic achievement of secondary school children in relation to gender and socio-economic status variations;

- To find out difference if any in academic achievement and achievement motivation of secondary school children due to gender and socio-economic status variations;

- To establish relationship between achievement motivation and academic achievement of secondary school children with regard to gender and socio-economic status variations;

- To compare the contribution of achievement motivation to academic achievement in relation to gender and socio-economic status variations.

2.2 Hypotheses Formulated for the study

All the hypotheses have been formulated in null form because of its advantages in verification. The following hypotheses have been formulated considering all the variables of the study:

- *Ho-1*: There does not exist statistically significant difference in achievement motivation of higher secondary school children in relation to gender variation;

- *Ho- 2*: There does not exist statistically significant difference in achievement motivation of higher secondary school children due to socio-economic status variation;

- *Ho- 3*: There does not exist statistically significant difference in achievement motivation of boys and girls of higher secondary schools;

- *Ho- 4*: There does not exist statistically significant difference in academic achievement of boys and girls of higher secondary schools;

- *Ho- 5*: There does not exist significant relationship in achievement motivation and academic achievement of children due to gender variation;

- *Ho- 6*: There does not exist significant relationship in achievement motivation and academic achievement of children due to Socio Economic Status variations;

- *Ho- 7*: There does not exist any difference in predicting achievement motivation towards academic achievement due to gender and Socio Economic Status variations.

2.3 Operational definitions of the terms

<u>**Achievement Motivation**</u>: 'Achievement Motivation' here is sensed as the attitude towards academic success along the line of Mehta (1969) where the student has to respond to a statement contained in a projective type of test, where it is conceived in terms of Thematic appreceptive measure. It is the tendency to strive for success and to choose goal oriented success/ failure activities. Here it refers to the scores obtained by the students on achievement motivation scale of Mehta (1969).

<u>**Academic Achievement**</u> : 'Academic Achievement' is conceived here as the achievement of the students in their 10th class Board Examination conducted by CBSE' 2006. As the examination maintains uniformity in standard evaluating procedure, curriculum, the marks obtained by the students are considered to have possessed higher validity and reliability evidences.

<u>**Gender:**</u> 'Gender' refers to boys and girls reading in higher secondary schools.

<u>**Socio- Economic Status:**</u> 'Socio-economic status' refers to the educational, occupational and income-wise standard of the parents of the sample.

2.4 Scope and limitations of the study

The scope of this study is limited to the extent of measuring the impact of achievement motivation by a projective technique and the academic performance at class X examination of students studying in class XI in higher secondary schools. The geographic locale is also same as the students from Gangtok city only have been considered as sample for the study. Age factor has been controlled as students belong to the same class.

The study is limited to only the Government and Private schools of Gangtok city selected on a simple random basis.

CHAPTER THREE

METHODOLOGY

1. *Design*

This study is mainly a descriptive study design of relationship study type. Relationship between achievement motivation and academic performance of the secondary school children in relation to sex, socio-economic status has been established without giving any input. Therefore, it is mainly an ex-post-facto type. Achievement motivation is the independent variable and academic performance is the dependant variable. The historical study design has not been adopted in the context of the nature of research. Because historical method is suitable for a research study that has interest in analyzing a phenomenon, event or condition in the context of forces and factors that operated in the past. For this reason, Primary and Secondary sources of data as well as internal and external evidences are required. But the present research work is not a developmental study since it aimed at investigating the factors influencing the dependent variable under the present conditions.

Application of experimental method of research was not thought to be suitable because of its objectives. This method is used in a research study that analyses the effects of predictors on the criterion variable under controlled situations.

Contrasted with historical or experimental design, descriptive designs are more specific in that they direct attention to particular aspects or dimensions of the research target. The heuristic value of descriptive studies must be considered a major contribution as well. Consistent with at least one of the objectives of research designs outlined by *Selltiz et al.(1959, p.50)*, descriptive studies can reveal potential relationships between variables, thus setting the stage for more elaborate investigation later.

3.2 Sample

For the purpose of this study the sample has been drawn from both Government schools and Private schools situated at Gangtok city.

The procedure for the selection of the sample has been adopted as follows. From among the English medium schools of Gangtok city students were selected from class XI. The students' strength of this class XI from five different high schools was 950 in number. A sample of 100 students from among them was selected on simple random basis. The detailed descriptions of the sample have been presented in a Table 1 below:

Table 1: *Selection of the sample*

3.3 Tools used for the study

The tools used for this study are:

- Mehta's Achievement Motivation Inventory (1969);
- School Achievement Record for taking scores on Academic Achievement;
- Socio Economic status scale of Nayak (2005).

1. *Mehta's Achievement Motivation inventory*

The achievement motivation inventory was developed by *Prayag Mehta (1969)*. The inventory is meant for secondary school children. It contains 22 items with 6 alternatives of which the respondents are required to check one. It is time bound inventory and 30 minutes only have been prescribed for attempting the same. Out of 6 alternatives, 2 are achievement related, 2 are task related and rest are unrelated achievement. For attempting a particular item, the photographs are first of all shown to the students and questions pertaining to the corresponding photograph are asked. Examples of such questions are illustrated below:

A boy is sitting on a cot. He has a book in his hand. An almirah full of books is lying nearby.

i.   He is preparing questions suggested by his teacher for the forth coming examination. (........)

ii. He is trying to find out the meaning of that word which no one in the class could explain. (........)

iii. He is looking at the coloured picture given in a book. (........)

iv. He is quickly doing the home task given by the teacher. (........)

v.   He is thinking about a new application of the principles given in a book. (........)

vi. He is reading a story. (........).

Out of these 6 options, (ii) and (v) are achievement related; (i) and (IV) are task related and (iii) and (VI) are unrelated. Because the response to any one item can be either achievement related, task related or unrelated. The options considered appropriate to the student may be any of these three. Because the respondent is required to check only one option. The score may relate to either achievement related or task related or unrelated. Few more examples of such questions are mentioned below:

A boy is reading a picture.

i.   He is thinking whether to complete the picture or to leave it unfinished. (........)

ii. He is practicing to make pictures. (........)

iii. He is making a picture to participate in the annual art competition to be held in the school. (........)

iv. He is thinking whether he should colour the picture. (........)

v.   He is learning the art of making pictures. (........)

vi. He is thinking that when he will have learned drawing well, then he would make beautiful pictures. (........)

A boy is holding a model of an aeroplane and is looking at it.

i.   He is thinking of becoming an engineer. (........)

ii. He is guessing the price of the aeroplane. (........)

iii. He is observing as to how the aeroplane has been made. (........)

iv. He is carefully checking the aeroplane before demonstrating his flying skill. (........)

v.   He is waiting for his friend so that he can get the aeroplane started by him. (........)

vi. He is thinking of repairing the damaged aeroplane. (........)

Two boys are standing, facing the mountains.

i.   They are enjoying the beauty of nature. (........)

ii. They are planning to climb up to the highest peak of the mountain. (........)

iii. They are studying the herbs available on the mountain. (........)
iv. They have become tired after a lot of walking and are just relaxing. (........)
v. They are thinking about the new techniques of mountaineering. (........)
vi. They are thinking of writing a report after having inspected the mountainous region. (........).

A farmer's son is ploughing the field.

i. He is contributing his share to make up the deficit of food in the country. (........)
ii. He is thinking of sowing after he has ploughed the land. (........)
iii. He is trying to get the maximum possible yield from his land. (........)
iv. He is ploughing the land to get sufficient food for himself and his family. (........)
v. He is ploughing the field to sow seeds. (........)
vi. He is using chemical fertilizers to make the land more productive. (........)

The validity of the scale was written by **Mehta (1961)** in form of theoretical validation and the reliability of the scale was measured in the form of internal consistency by Kuder- Richardson and Split – Half methods. The values of KR-20 reliability co-efficient were 0.67 and Split half reliability was found to be 0.55.

The response to each of the item in terms of achievement related, task related and unrelated has been provided by the investigator. So scoring key for the inventory is shown in the table 2 in following page:

Table 2: *Scoring key for the inventory*

3.3.2 School achievement record for measuring academic achievement

So far as academic performance is concerned in the present investigation, the investigator has considered the final marks of class X examination of the student as the academic performance score because the examination is conducted under similar conditions, uniform curriculum, same questions, and uniform scoring procedure. The final marks obtained by the students in class X has been converted to percentages and accepted in terms of whole numbers omitting the decimals fractions as for example if the student score is 71.5 *per cent* his percentage mark is taken as 73. But had it been 72.4 *per cent*, it is reckoned as 72 *per cent* only. The percentage had been calculated from the aggregate marks of the students.

3.3.3 Socio-economic status scale of Nayak (2005)

The SES scale of *Nayak (2005)* has been adopted to study SES status of the parents of the children. The scale constitutes of there parts education, Occupation and Income. Each of these categories have 9 sub-categories. The total score of the sub-categories checked in each criteria show the SES of the subject. The description of the SES scale is given here under:

SES scale of Nayak (weightage of items appear in parenthesis)

A: Personal background data

(i) Name

(ii) Name of your father

(iii) Name of your mother

(iv) Number of person in your family

(v) Nature of family – nuclear/ Joint.

(vi) Age

(vii) Caste

(viii) Gender

B: Education

Educational qualification of your father / mother

IAS/ CA/ MBA/ CS: [10]

SAS/ Engineer/ Medical: [09]

MA/ M Sc/ M Com/ LLM: [08]

BA/ B Sc/ B Com/ LLB: [07]

IA/ I Sc/ I Com: [06]

H SCE/ H SC: [05]

Middle school level: [04]

Primary level: [03]

Illiterate: [02]

C: Occupation

Indicate what the occupation of your father / mother is

Administrative Service: [10]

Company services: [09]

Engineer/ Doctor: [08]

College Teachers: [06]

Clerical: [06]

Workers: [05]

Skilled: [04]

Non-skilled: [03]

Unemployed: [02]

D: Income

Above Rs. 50,000: [10]
Rs. 40,000 to Rs. 49,999: [09]
Rs. 30,000 to Rs. 39,999: [08]
Rs. 20,000 to Rs. 29,999: [07]
Rs. 10,000 to Rs. 19,999: [06]
Rs. 1,000 to Rs. 9,999: [05]
Below Rs. 1,000: [04]
Material wealth: [03]
Building: [02]

Total Score	SES
16 – 29	High
> 16	Low

The validity and reliability of the scale is determined where the retest reliability co-efficient was found to be 0.07 and concurrent validity co-efficient is 0.61.

3.4 Techniques of Data Analysis

The following techniques have been used for this study:

- *Questionnaire technique for collection of data;*
- *Descriptive measures for ascertaining relative standing of the sample on different variables;*
- *Inferential statistics for determining significance of difference between the sub- sample;*
- *Measures of relationship between the variables.*

3.5 Procedure

Procedures adopted for obtaining data, its analysis and interpretation is delineated below:

- *Administration of the questionnaire are a sample of 100 secondary school students selected on simple random basis;*
- *Scoring as per manuals;*

- *Data collection-scores has been tabulated on a data sheet according to the variables under study;*
- *Intra-variable analysis have been made through 't' test;*
- *Relationship study has been conducted by co-relating Socio Economic Status score with achievement motivation scores;*
- *Interpretation of results was made as per the value obtained from calculation;*
- *At last, a brief summary has been given along with recommendations.*

CHAPTER FOUR

RESULTS AND DISCUSSIONS

In the section, attempts have been made to present the data along with analysis of the same. For this, the questionnaire was administered first and then scoring was made for descriptive and differential analysis in accordance with the objectives and hypothesis formulated before hand.

4.1 Administration of the scale

For administration of the scale over a sample of 100 students of class XI selected at random. The principles of administering a questionnaire are strictly followed. They are described as follows:

- The investigator first of all sought for the permission of the administration of the same from the Head of the institution;
- Rapport was established between the investigator and the students and it was made clear to the students that neither it is meant for examining them nor for utilizing the same for any other purpose rather then research;
- The students who agreed to the proposal sat for the administration of the questionnaire;
- Preliminary consideration for administration of a questionnaire were made like free ventilation, good sitting accommodation and undisturbed zone of the institution;
- A placard containing 'Don't Disturb' was hung on the door of the examination hall;
- Students were given all information and clarifications for responding of the items of the scale;
- The time-period for administration was chosen in such a way so that there was no possibility for any disturbance i,e. The time fixed for

administration was neither before or after lunch nor before or after any amusement activity;

- All the students were provided with answers sheets & pencils;
- They were told to record their responses on the spaces specified for the purpose along with all general information sought for the same;
- They were requested to complete the assignment within an hour even though there was no fixed time for the same.

4.1.1 Scoring of the Answer sheet

The Answer-sheets were collected and scored as per the manual. It was a six- choiced scale out of which 2 options were 'task related', 2 'unrelated' and 2 'achievement related'. As per the objectives of the study, only the achievement related score was found out as per the manual.

4.1.2 Distribution of the Achievement Motivation scores

The Scores were then compiled in the according order and the highest score as well as the lowest score was found out. It ranged from 1-18 in case of boys and 1-15 in case of girls.

The descriptive statistics procedures were then followed for analyzing the scores. The following distribution of scores is presented as for the variations:

Table 3: *Frequency of distribution of scores on Achievement Motivation scale of the total sample and the sub samples of sex (Gender) and SES (Socio Economic Status).*

C.I	Boys	Girls	Total	HSES	LSES	Total
16-18	1	0	01	0	0	0
13-15	0	1	01	0	0	0
10-12	16	16	32	06	04	10
7-9	18	21	39	13	13	26
4-6	7	16	23	03	05	08
1-3	1	3	04	02	01	03
Total	43	57	100	24	23	47

From the frequency distribution descriptive measures like mean, Standard Deviation were calculated for interpretation of result through verification of null hypothesis. The result is presented in the Table 4 below:

Table 4: *Distribution of scores on achievement motivation scale*

CI	F	CF	x		Fx	Fx2
16-18	01	100	+03	+ 03		09
13-15	01	99	+02	+ 02		04
10-12	32	98	+01	+ 32	+ 37	32
07-09	39	66	0	0		0
04-06	23	27	- 01	- 23		23
01-03	04	04	- 02	- 08	- 31	16
Total	100				Σ Fx= 06	Σ Fx2= 84

Mean = 8.18; Median = 8.26; Standard Deviation = 2.73

From the above table, it is evident that the mean of the total sample is 8.18 and median is 8.26 showing thereby that the scores fall almost within the limitations of normal probability curve. Maximum students fall within the class interval 7- 9 with abrupt tapering towards the higher and lower end. The maximum concentration has been within the class interval of 4-12 indicating that the most of them have medium level of achievement motivation.

On scrutiny of the scores for studying normality of the scores, the skew ness and kurtosis values were calculated. The values were - .09 and .27 respectively as against 0 and 0.263 for a normal curve. From the result, the investigator desires to conclude that the scores obtained by the students on achievement motivation scale deviates slightly from the normal distribution so far as Kurtosis is concerned but on the whole the distribution is negatively skewed and little bit platy kurtic as can be seen from the figure below:

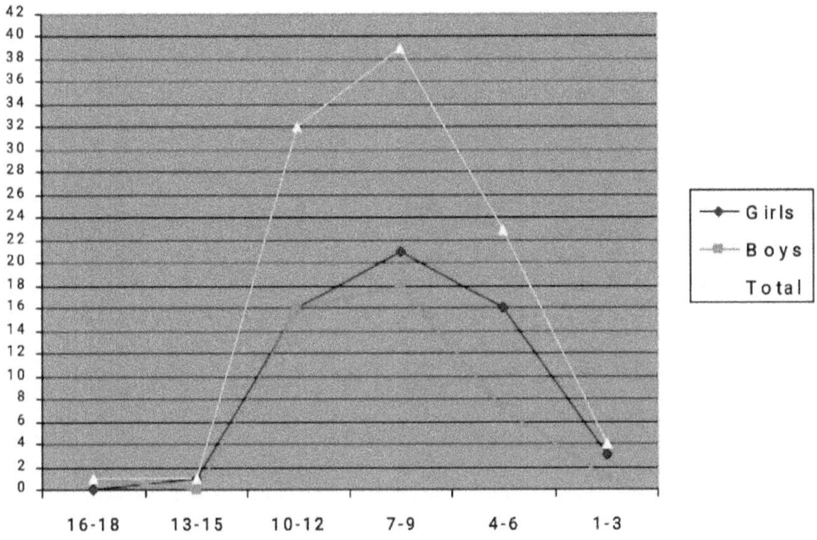

Figure 1: Study of Normality of distribution of scores on Achievement Motivation Scale

4.1.3 Descriptive measures on achievement motivation scale

The entire sample along with its sub-samples were subjected the study of descriptive measures like mean and standard deviation for interpretation of results. The sample was split into sub-samples according to two variations like sex and socio-economic status. As such, the following sub-samples have been obtained:

Sex	Boys
Sex variationSex	Girls
Socio-economic status (SES) variation	High SES
	Low SES

The mean and standard deviation of the total sample alongwith the sub-samples have been calculated and presented in table 5 below:

Table 5: *Mean and Standard deviation of Total sample, sub-samples of sex and SES variations*

Variation		N	M	SD
Sex	Boys	43	8.69	0.87
	Girls	57	7.79	0.84
SES	HSES	24	7.87	0.78
	LSES	23	7.61	0.69
Total		100	8.18	2.73

After calculating the Mean and Standard Deviation, the test of significance of difference between the means of the contrast was calculated to find out the significance of difference between two contrasts. The result is presented in Table 6 below:

Table 6: *Test of significance of difference between the mean scores on Achievement Motivation scale due to Sex and SES variations*

Variation		N	M	SD	df	't'
Sex	Boys	43	8.69	0.87		
	Girls	57	7.79	0.84	98	5.3
SES	HSES	24	7.87	0.78		
	LSES	23	7.61	0.69	45	1.2

't' for df 98 critical value=2.63; 't' = 5.3; Hence þ < 0.01.

It was observed that the 't' ratio in case of sex variations was significant because 't' for df 98 requires a critical value of 2.63 as the calculated 't' ratio is greater than the table value of 't'. The 't' ratio is considered significant, therefore, the null hypothesis that there does not exist significant difference in the Mean score of achievement motivation due to sex variation is rejected. The study shows that boys are more achievement motivation oriented compared to girls.

In case of SES variations the 't' ratio could not be significant therefore the null hypothesis that there does not exist significant difference in achievement motivation score due to SES variations could not be rejected which shows that SES does not play any role in the achievement motivation of the students.

The study is in conformity with earlier studies conducted by The study is in conformity with earlier studies conducted by *Mohanty (1998), Ahluwalia (1985), Chauhan (1984), Vimla (1985), Chatterji, S., Mukherjee, M and Banerjee, S.N (1971)* who have shown sex as an intervening variable for achievement motivation.

However sex variations and SES variations was also considered as not influencing achievement motivation in the studies of *Abrol (1977), Ghuman (1978), Jerath (1979) and Gandhi (1982).* Considering the above the investigator desires to conclude that the result obtained in the present study is appropriate.

4.2 Collection of data regarding academic performance

Data has been collected regarding academic performance from the school achievement record of class 10th. As the Board examination maintains uniformity in standard evaluating procedure, curriculum, the marks obtained by the students are considered to have possessed higher validity and reliability evidences.

4.2.1 Distribution of the Academic performance scores

The Scores were then compiled in the ascending order and the highest score as well as the lowest score was found out. It ranged from 48 - 85 in case of boys and 40 - 87 in case of girls.

The descriptive statistics procedures were then followed for analyzing the scores. The following distribution of scores is presented as for the variations in the table 7 below:

Table 7: *Frequency of distribution of scores on academic performance of the total samples and the sub-samples*

CI	Boys	Girls	Total
85 -89	1	1	2
80 – 84	6	2	8
75 – 79	8	2	10
70 – 74	11	2	13
65 – 69	7	5	12
60 – 64	4	6	10
55 – 59	2	13	15
50 – 54	2	14	16
45 – 49	2	8	10
40 – 44	0	4	4
Total	43	57	100

From the frequency distribution descriptive measures like Mean and Stadard Deviation were calculated for interpretation of result through verification of null hypothesis. The result is presented in the Table 8 below:

Table 8: *Distribution of scores on academic performance*

CI	F	CF	X	Fx		FX2
85 -89	2	100	+ 7	+ 14		98
80 – 84	8	98	+ 6	+48		288
75 – 79	10	90	+ 5	+ 50		250
70 – 74	13	80	+ 4	+ 52	235	208
65 – 69	12	67	+ 3	+ 36		108
60 – 64	10	55	+ 2	+ 20		40
55 – 59	15	45	+ 1	+ 15		15
50 – 54	16	30	0	0		0
45 – 49	10	14	- 1	- 10	- 18	10
40 – 44	0	04	- 2	- 08		16
	N =100			Σ Fx= 217		Σ Fx2= 1033

Mean = 62.84; Median = 60.75; Standard Deviation = 11.85

From the above table it is evident that the Mean of the total sample is 62.84 and the Median is 60.75 showing thereby that the scores fall almost within the limitation of normal probability curve. Maximum students fall within the class interval 50 - 54 with abrupt tapering towards the higher and lower ends. The maximum concentration has been within the class interval of 45 - 59 indicating that the most of them have medium level of academic performance.

On scrutiny of the scores for studying normality of the scores, the skew ness and kurtosis values were calculated. The values were 0.62 and 0.268 respectively as against 0 and 0.263 for a normal curve. From the result, the investigator desires to conclude that the scores obtained by the students on academic performance deviates slightly from the normal distribution so far as Kurtosis is concerned but on the whole the distribution is positively skewed and little bit platy kurtic as can be seen from the graph below:

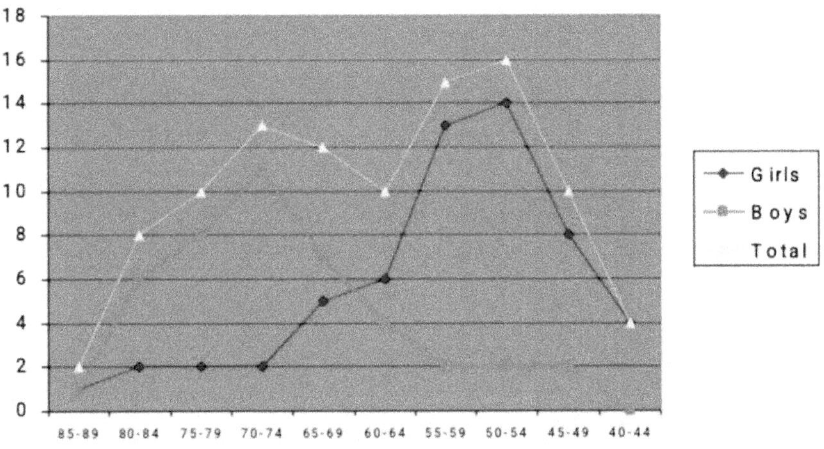

Figure 2: Study of Normality of Distribution of scores on Academic Performance

4.2.2 Descriptive measures on academic performance

The entire sample along with its sub-samples were subjected the study of descriptive measures like mean and standard deviation for interpretation of results. The sample was split into sub-samples according to two variations like sex and socio-economic status. As such, the following sub-samples have been obtained:

Sex	Boys
Sex variationSex	Girls
Socio-economic status (SES) variation	High SES
	Low SES

The mean and standard deviation of the total sample alongwith the sub-samples have been calculated and presented in table 9 below:

Table 9: *Mean and Standard deviation of Total sample, sub-samples of sex and SES variations*

Variation		N	M	SD
Sex	Boys	43	70.14	9.55
	Girls	57	57.35	10.30
SES	HSES	24	7.87	0.78
	LSES	23	7.61	0.69
Total		100	62.84	11.85

After calculating the Mean and Standard Deviation, the test of significance of difference between the means of the contrast was calculated to find out the significance of difference between two contrasts. The result is presented in Table 10 below:

Table 10: *Test of significance of difference between the mean scores on Academic performance due to Sex and SES variations*

Variation		N	M	SD	df	't'
Sex	Boys	43	70.14	9.55		
	Girls	57	57.35	10.30	98	6.06
SES	HSES	24	7.87	0.78		
	LSES	23	7.61	0.69	45	1.2

't' for df 98 critical value=2.63; 't' = 6.06; Hence þ < 0.01.

It was observed that the 't' ratio in case of sex variations was significant because 't' for df 98 requires a critical value of 2.63 as the calculated 't' ratio is greater than the table value of 't'. The 't' ratio is considered significant, therefore, the null hypothesis that there does not exist significant difference in the Mean score of academic performance due to sex variation is rejected. The study shows that boys are more academic performance oriented compared to girls.

In case of SES variations the 't' ratio could not be significant therefore the null hypothesis that there does not exist significant difference in academic performance score due to SES variations could not be rejected which shows that SES does not play any role in the academic performance of the students. The study is in conformity with earlier studies conducted by

Abrol (1977), Ghuman (1978) and *Gandhi (1982).* Considering the above the investigator desires to conclude that the result obtained in the present study is appropriate.

4.3Relationship study between Achievement motivation Vs. SES and Achievement motivation Vs. Academic Achievement.

Relationship study was established through product moment correlation sub-sample - wise and total – wise. The result is presented in Table 11 below:

Table 11: *Relationship between Achievement Motivation (AM) Vs. SES and Achievement Motivation Vs. Academic Achievement (AA)*

Sample	AM vs. SES [r]	AM Vs. AA [r]
Boys	0.01	0.01
Girls	0.01	0.03
Total	0.28	0.18

It was observed that relationship between Achievement motivation and socio Economic status in case of boys is negligible and in case of girls is also negligible but in total it is significant.

Relationship between achievement motivation and academic achievement in case of boys is negligible and in case of girls is also negligible while in total case it is significant.

Therefore, the null hypotheses that there does not exist significant relationship in achievement motivation and academic achievement of children due to sex variation could not be rejected which shows that sex variation does not play any role in the relationship of achievement motivation and academic achievement. But in toto achievement motivation is related to academic performance.

CHAPTER FIVE

SUMMARY AND RECOMMENDATIONS

5.1 The Summary

In the present competitive world everybody desires for a high level of achievement. Quality of performance has been regarded as a key factor for personal progress and national development. Such a desire for high level of achievement emphasizes on the educational system in a larger perspective which has raised several questions for educational researchers in respect of factors contributing and promoting academic achievement. Educational researchers all over the world are still seeking a breakthrough in elucidating this phenomenon. A synoptic review of the researchers conducted so far have highlighted academic achievement in relation to certain inherent variables such as teaching variables, sociological variables and psycho social variables. On the whole, the importance on both cognitive and non-cognitive aspects as co-relates to academic achievement have been highlighted in the same quantum.

Intelligence, anxiety, values, interest, aptitudes, self concepts, study habits, achievement motivation are regarded as the inherent variables for academic achievement. Achievement motivation as a factor in relation to academic achievement has been found out by Mitra (1985), Sharma (1981) and many others. This impact of psycho social variables on academic achievement has been the main area of research from the time immemorial. The present study has focused on achievement motivation as the co-relates of academic achievement.

Achievement motivation has been considered as an extended person-intrinsic motivation showing a pattern of actions, planning and feelings connected with striving to achieve some internalized standards of excellence. Need for achievement has been regarded as an individual's personality affecting person's behaviour. It is also regarded as a learned motivation. Individuals with high need for achievement are entrusted in this case. Excellence is the catch word behind considering achievement motivation as a variable for the study.

Tripathy (1986) has studied achievement motivation and its co-relates by showing significant relationship of two variables. The study has been confirmed by *Singh (1986) Ahluwalia (1985)* and *Chauhan (1984).*

As academic achievement is not a function of cognitive variable alone the emphatic stress on the contribution of psycho social variable is imperative. As such, which of the psycho social variable is of prime importance, what percentage of proportion variance is attributable by them towards the criterion, needs elaboration and quantification. The present investigation is a noble attempt of the investigator in this area. Considering the importance of the non-cognitive variables effecting academic achievement, the present day trend in the system of education has been changed and in addition to the cognitive variables non -cognitive variables have been given due stress. Hence the rationale of the study is justified.

Objectives of the study

The objectives of the study are:

- *To ascertain achievement motivation of the students of secondary schools in relation to gender and socio- economic status variations;*
- *To determine the academic achievement of secondary school children in relation to gender and socio-economic status variations;*
- *To find out difference if any in academic achievement and achievement motivation of secondary school children due to gender and socio- economic status variations;*
- *To establish relationship between achievement motivation and academic achievement of secondary school children with regard to gender and socio-economic status variations;*
- To compare the contribution of achievement motivation to academic achievement in relation to gender and socio-economic status variations.

Hypotheses of the study

All the hypotheses have been formulated in null form because of its advantages in verification. The following hypotheses have been formulated considering all the variables of the study:

- **Ho-1**: There does not exist statistically significant difference in achievement motivation of higher secondary school children in relation to gender variation;
- **Ho- 2**: There does not exist statistically significant difference in achievement motivation of higher secondary school children due to socio-economic variation;
- **Ho- 3**: There does not exist statistically significant difference in achievement motivation of boys and girls of higher secondary schools;
- **Ho- 4**: There does not exist statistically significant difference in academic achievement of boys and girls of higher secondary schools;
- **Ho- 5**: There does not exist significant relationship in achievement motivation and academic achievement of children due to gender variation;
- **Ho- 6**: There does not exist significant relationship in achievement motivation and academic achievement of children due to Socio Economic Status variations;
- **Ho- 7**: There does not exist any difference in predicting achievement motivation towards academic achievement due to gender and Socio Economic Status variations.

Operational definitions of the terms

Achievement Motivation: 'Achievement Motivation' here is sensed as the attitude towards academic success along the line of Mehta (1969) where the student has to respond to a statement contained in a projective type of test, where it is conceived in terms of Thematic appreceptive measure. It is the tendency to strive for success and to choose goal oriented success/ failure activities. Here it refers to the scores obtained by the students on achievement motivation scale of Mehta (1969).

Academic Achievement : 'Academic Achievement' is conceived here as the achievement of the students in their 10th class Board Examination conducted by CBSE' 2006. As the examination maintains uniformity in standard evaluating procedure, curriculum, the marks obtained by the students are considered to have possessed higher validity and reliability evidences.

Gender: 'Gender' refers to boys and girls reading in higher secondary schools.

Socio- Economic Status: 'Socio-economic status' refers to the educational, occupational and income-wise standard of the parents of the sample.

Scope and limitations of the study

The scope of this study is limited to the extent of measuring the impact of achievement motivation by a projective technique and the academic performance at class X examination of students studying in class XI in higher secondary schools. The geographic locale is also same as the students from Gangtok city only have been considered as sample for the study. Age factor has been controlled as students belong to the same class.

The study is limited to only the Government and Private schools of Gangtok city selected on a simple random basis.

Method of the study

Design: This study is mainly a descriptive study design of relationship study type. Relationship between achievement motivation and academic performance of the secondary school children in relation to gender, socio-economic status and school intervention variation has been established without giving any input. Therefore, it is mainly an ex-post-facto type.

*Sample:*For the purpose of this study the sample size of 100 students from government and Private schools situated at Gangtok city has been selected on simple random basis.

Tools: The tools used for this study are:

- *Mehta's Achievement Motivation Inventory (1969);*
- *School Achievement Record for taking scores on Academic Achievement;*
- *Socio Economic status scale of Nayak (2005).*

Techniques of Data Analysis

The following techniques have been used for this study:

- Questionnaire technique for collection of data;
- Descriptive measures for ascertaining relative standing of the sample on different variables;
- Inferential statistics for determining significance of difference between the sub- sample;
- Measures of relationship between the variables.

The Findings

The study is mainly a co-relational study which includes both descriptive and inferential statistics. The result revealed that:

- *Boys are more achievement motivation oriented compared to girls;*
- *Socio economic status does not play any role in the achievement motivation of the students;*
- *Relationship between achievement motivation and socio economic status in case of girls is negligible;*
- *Relationship between achievement motivation and socio economic status in case of boys is negligible;*
- *Relationship between achievement motivation and academic achievement in case of boys is negligible;*
- *Relationship between achievement motivation and academic achievement in case of girls is negligible;*
- *Gender variation does not play any role in the relationship of achievement motivation and academic achievement.*

5.2 Recommendations

Achievement in its many and varied form has been, and remains, a topic of continuing concern for societies, institutions , groups and the individuals who compose them. The factors that result in achievement are many and varied, but it is widely assumed that one of the primary elements in all fields of achievement is motivation. This is true whether it is work, School or sport that is the particular focus of interest. In fact, of course, it is not only employers, leaders and teachers who are concerned with motivation but rather it is all of us in one or another of our life roles. It is, therefore, timely to look again at the factors which act positively or negatively upon motivation.

In the present day test- conscious age high academic achievement is the main motto. For this the cognitive variables like, intelligence, creativity, aptitude and affective characteristics like attitude, self concept, personality traits, level of aspiration, test, anxiety have been proved to be important predictors to the criterion of academic achievement. The present study is a replica of the above in respect of importance of psycho social variables and their significance in the field of achievement. As such the findings provide ample scope both to the administrators and the educationalists in promoting achievement and making parents, teachers, students and all other concerns well informed about the same. The following recommendations have been made basing on the findings of the present investigation:

- **Importance of psycho social variables in the field of academic achievement**

Quality of performance being regarded as a key factor for national development desire for high level of academic achievement is on full swing. As education refines, reconstructs and redesigns the needs according to the demands, the high priority has been given to Psycho social variables along with the cognitive variables because a desire for learning, an attitudinal bent of mind with proper appreciation and interest for a particular work can only be beneficial. Therefore, the investigator desires to recommend for provision of psycho social variables in the school curriculum in a rigorous way as examinable subjects carry weightage to these variables should wisely be formulated and incorporated in the curriculum. In this context, redesigning policy on education (1986) is found to be befitting and conductive for the sake of greater public interest.

- **Development of need to achieve**

Achievement motivation is one of the most important Psycho social variables of this study. From the present study it has been found that need achievement has perfect positive relationship with academic achievement. So in order to raise the academic achievement of the students, it is essential to develop their achievement motivation. Therefore, the situations in the home and in the school should promote the need achievement of the pupil. In the context of the result in the present investigation the following recommendations have been made:

(i) Emphasis on intellectual pursuit

Need achievement can be raised if the students develop their level of intelligence. Level of intelligence can be raised by encouraging the students to develop the problem solving ability, thinking ,reasoning etc. by participating in different activities and studying the creative work of different persons. So, for the development of achievement motivation among the students the intellectual development should be promoted.

The school should organize different curricular and co-curricular activities like seminars, talks delivered by the intellectuals, debates, discussions, etc and should also promote students to gain correct and current information, by studying the magazines, newspapers, journals, periodicals. It should encourage the students to study the creative writing of the eminent scholars. Not only the whole responsibility goes to the School and teachers for promoting achievement motivation but also the home, parents, elders, neighbours share a lot. Parents should give the answers to each of the questions of their children with a great patience. They should maintain home atmosphere proper for the children's intellectual pursuit.

(ii) Affectionate parental behaviour

Achievement motivation is also influenced by the parental behaviour. Parents should be affectionate enough. They should listen and understand all the queries, problems and needs of their children and should try to solve them but they should not be over affectionate which is fraught with the risk of spoiling their children. They should encourage the children to meet each and every problem of their life.

(iii)Permissiveness of parents

Parents should be permissive. They should encourage the children to know, to gain information by participating in different life situation. They should encourage them to be flexible, fearless and perceive the correct knowledge only after the scientific and objective investigation.

- **Development of level of aspiration**

Pupils should have high level of aspiration. High level of aspiration is responsible for developing high need achievement. The teachers and the parents should set high goals before the students so that they should try to achieve them and they should develop the tendency to achieve more and more. But care must be taken that the goals should be set up by keeping an eye to the age, sex, intellectual standard and habitational variable or else it will have negative impact upon the children and may block their achievement.

- **Reducing frustration reactions**

Need achievement is also hampered by frustration. Frustration results from repeated failure in any activities. The process of blocking or thwarting needs causes frustration in human beings. If the children repeatedly fail in any activities they develop frustration reactions, which block their motive to achieve. So the children should be encouraged to develop their patience and to continue the activity until the success is achieved.

- **Removal of prejudices and biases**

Conservative attitudes, prejudices attached to different situations and objects are responsible in reducing the achievement motivation. The attitude of the people attached with the resistance of girls education, caste system, child marriages, pre conceived ideas about the quantity and quality of education often cause to reduce the achievement motivation in students. So, care must be taken to free the society from these prejudices and biases.

- **Level of concept acquisition is to be highlighted**

Teacher should make the concept clear before the students for which they are striving. Pupil should know about the problems and prospects of the concept, the idea so that they should try in different ways to achieve the same. So, for the development of achievement motivation the level of concept acquisition is to be highlighted.

- **Better scope for training for enhancing achievement motivation**

Achievement motivation can also be enhanced by properly planned training programme. Workshops, training, refresher courses, inservices training courses should be provided for the teachers to help them to equip with necessary skills and competencies to enhance students' achievement motivation.

- **Development of socio cultural status**

Socio cultural status also influences the achievement motivation of the students. Different society and cultural groups have their own goal, standard or criterion. The pupil from these groups, represent their society and culture and try to achieve and stick to their own goal, standard or criterion. So, if the socio cultural status can be improved the achievement motivation of the pupil can also be improved.

Over and above, for higher achievement motivation the meaningful, joyful experience in the educational level will lead to greater satisfaction and the greater utility value of the system of education will develop the strongest base for achievement motivation. Hence need specific and utility specific educational system will very highly be appreciated. The system and method of curriculum having more scope for job opportunities will also be the great source for developing need to achieve motive in students.

Bibliography

Abrol, D. N. (1977): A Study of Achievement Motivation in relation to Intelligence, Vocational interest, Achievement, Sex and Socio economic status. In M.B. Buch (Edited) Third Survey of Research in Education (P.317), New Delhi: NCERT.

Anand, S.P. & Dave, P.N. (1979): A Trend Report on Correlates of Achievement. In M.B. Buch (Edited), Fourth survey of Research in Education, New Delhi: NCERT.

Ahluwalia, I. (1985): A Study of Factors Affecting Achievement Motivation. In M.B. Buch (Edited) Fourth Survey of Research in Education (P. 333), New Delhi: NCERT.

Ames, C. (1992): Classroom goals, structures, and student motivation. Journal of Educational Psychology, 84 (3), 261-271.

Buch, M.B. (1972): A survey of Research in Educational psychology.

Burger, J. M. (1997): Personality Pacific Grove, CA: Brooks /cole Pu.

Chatterji, P.S. (1983): A comparative study of personality, Intelligence and Achievement motivation of students in different academic groups. In M. B. Buch (Edited) Fourth Survey of Research in Education (p. 351), New Delhi: NCERT.

Chauhan, S. S. (1984): A comparative study of the Achievement motivation of scheduled Tribe and scheduled castes students of Himachal Pradesh in relation to their Intelligence and Socio- economic status. In M.B. Buch (Edited) Fourth survey of Research in Education (p 354, 355), New Delhi: NCERT.

Dweck, C. (1986): Motivational processes affecting learning. American Psychologist. 41 (10), 1040-1048.

Farmer, H.S. (1985): Variables related to career commitment, mastery motivation, and level of career aspiration among college students. Journal of Career Development, 21 (4), p. 265-278.

Ghuman M. S. (1976): A study of aptitudes, personality traits and Achievement motivation of academic over- Achievers and under – achieves. In M. B. Buch (Edited) Third survey of Research in Education (PP 664, 665), New Delhi: NCERT.

Gupta, J. P (1978): A study of anxiety and Achievement motivation in relation to Academic Achievement, Sex and Economic Status. In M. B. Buch (Edited) Third Survey of Research in Education (P. 356), New Delhi:

NCERT.

Gupta, P. L. (1983): A study of personality characteristics of Ninth grade over and under achievement boys and girls at different levels of Achievement Motivation. In M.B. Buch (Edited) Fourth Survey of Research in Education (P.370), New Delhi: NCERT.

Hussain, M. G. (1979): Recall of Finished and Interrupted Tasks under Ego and Task- oriented conditions in relation to Anxiety, Need Achievement and Need for Approval motive and personality variables. In M.B. Buch (Edited) Third Survey of Research in Education (PP 359,360), New Delhi: NCERT.

Jerath, J. M. (1979): A study of Achievement Motivation and its personality Motivation and ability correlates. In M. B. Buch (Edited) Fourth survey of Research in Education (P.375), New Delhi: NCERT.

Jain, S. (1983): Concept Formation as a Function of verbal Intelligence and Achievement Motivation. In M.B. Buch (Edited) Fourth survey of Research in Education (P.374), New Delhi: NCERT.

Murray, H. (1938): Explorations in Personality. New York: Oxford University Press.

McClelland, D. C., Atkinson, J. W.; Clark, R. A and Howell, E.L. (1953): The Achievement Motive, New York. Appleton Century crafts.

McClelland, D. C. (1958): Risk- taking in children with high and low needs for achievement. In Atkinson J. W. (edited) 1958. Motives is Fantasy, Action and society, Toronto: Van Nostrand.

McClelland, D. C. (1961): The Achieving society. Princepton, N. J. Van Nostrand.

Mohanty, P (1998): Comparative role of self concept, Achievement Motivation and test anxiety as predictors to academic achievement. Unpublished. Ph.D Dissertation in Education, Utkal University.

Maslow, A. (1954): Motivation and personality New York: Harper.

Mukherjee, B. N. (1969): Prediction of grades in Introductory Psychology from the Taylor Manifest Anxiety scale using a Multivariate Covariance Adjustment Method. In M. B Buch (Edited) Third survey of Research in Education, New Delhi: NCERT.

Mehta, P. (1969): The Achievement Motive in High School Boys, New Delhi: NCERT.

Narula, K. S. (1979): A Study of Achievement Motivation, Personal preferences, Perception, Anxiety, Risk taking behaviour and other correlates in relation to Intelligence, Socio-economic status and performance of the prospective secondary School Teachers of Orissa State. In M.B. Buch (Edited) Third survey of Research in Education (PP 385-386), New Delhi: NCERT.

Nayak, S. (2004): Level of aspiration, Achievement motivation and academic achievement of higher secondary pupils in relation to sex and socio-economic status, unpublished Ph. D dissertation, Utkal University.

Patel, R. M. (1981): A study of general ability as a predicator of academic achievement of the pupils of standards II, III and IV. In M. B. Buch (Edited) Third Survey of Research in Education, New Delhi: NCERT.

Raghava, (1985): A Study of Achievement Motivation Development in the pupils of Ninth standard with various Socio-Economic levels and studying the effects thereof; Ph.D. Edu; Mys. U.

Rajeeva, M. (1982): A study of Achievement Motive, its correlates and performance of IX grade pupils of secondary schools of Bangalore. In M.B. Buch (Edited) Third Survey of Research in education (P. 399), New Delhi: NCERT.

Sharma, R. R. (1979): Self concept, level of Aspiration and mental health as factors in Academic Achievement. In M.B. Buch (Edited) Third Survey of Research in Education, New Delhi: NCERT.

Shivappa. D. (1980): A Study on Factors affecting the academic achievement of high school pupils. In M.B Buch (Edited) Third Survey of Research in Education, New Delhi; NCERT.

Sheel, A. P (1981): Task Performance as a function of n-Achievement, Anxiety and creativity among Male and Female Adolescents. In M. B. Buch (Edited) Third Survey of Research in Education (P-414), New Delhi: NCERT.

Singh, V. (1981): Anxiety and Need Achievement in relation taster's Set. In M. B. Buch (Edited) Third Survey of Research in Education (P.423), New Delhi: NCERT.

Teevan, R. C & Mc. Ghee, P.E (1972): Childhood development of fear and failure motivation. Journal of personality and social Psychology (PP 345. 348).

Tripathi, R. C. (1986): Achievement Motivation and its correlates of high school student of East U.P. In M.B. Buch (Edited) Fourth Survey of Research in Education, (PP. 452-453), New Delhi: NCERT.

Urdan, T., & Maehr, M. (1995): Beyond a two- goal theory of motivation and achievement: A case for social goals Review of Educational research, 65(3), 213-243.

Vidler, D. C. (1977): Achievement Motivation: In Ball, S. (Edited) Motivation in Education (1977) (PP-67-90) New York: Academic press.

Vats, A. (1980): Biochemical correlates of Scholastics Achievement, Achievement Motivation Creative Functioning and Anxiety, In M. B. Buch (Edited) Third Survey of Research in Education (PP. 696.697), New Delhi: NCERT.

Wurterbottom, M. R. (1958): The relation of need for Achievement to learning experience in independence and mastery. In J.W. Atkinson (Edited) Motives in Fantasy, Action and Society Princeton, N.J Van Nostrand.

Zargar, A. H. (1980): A study of Expression Neuroticism and n-Achievement in relation to Intelligence, creativity and Scholastic Achievement. In M.B Buch (Edited) Third Survey of Research in Education (p.439), New Delhi; NCERT.

Appendices

Mehta's achievement motivation inventory (1969)

DIRECTIONS

We are interested in measuring your achievement motivation in academics. To facilitate this exercise, a questionnaire with 22 test items has been prepared. Each of the test items questionnaires has six options to be responded by you. You are requested to fill only one option you consider to be most appropriate. Besides, please also note the following:

- Please note that only one tick mark should be put under only one choice for one question.
- Please make sure that you give your response for all items without leaving any item blank.
- This is not ability test and there is no right or wrong answers. This is only an attempt to evaluate your achievement motivation.
- Do not spend too much time on one statement. Give the first and the best response that comes to your mind on reading each of the statement.
- Be honest and frank in giving your responses.
- Please do not change once you mark your option.

1. *A boy is sitting on a cot. He has a book in his hand. An almirah full of books is lying nearby.*

    i. He is preparing questions suggested by his teacher for the forth coming examination. (........).
    ii. He is trying to find out the meaning of that word which no one in the class could explain. (........).
    iii. He is looking at the coloured picture given in a book. (........).
    iv. He is quickly doing the home task given by the teacher. (........).
    v. He is thinking about a new application of the principles given in a book. (........).
    vi. He is reading a story. (........).

1. *A boy is reading a picture.*

   i. He is thinking whether to complete the picture or to leave it unfinished. (........).
   ii. He is practicing to make pictures. (........).
   iii. He is making a picture to participate in the annual art competition to be held in the school. (........).
   iv. He is thinking whether he should colour the picture. (........).
   v. He is learning the art of making pictures. (........).
   vi. He is thinking that when he will have learned drawing well, then he would make beautiful pictures. (........).

2. *A boy is holding a model of an aeroplane and is looking at it.*

   i. He is thinking of becoming an engineer. (........).
   ii. He is guessing the price of the aeroplane. (........).
   iii. He is observing as to how the aeroplane has been made. (........).
   iv. He is carefully checking the aeroplane before demonstrating his flying skill. (........).
   v. He is waiting for his friend so that he can get the aeroplane started by him. (........).
   vi. He is thinking of repairing the damaged aeroplane. (........).

3. *Two boys are standing, facing the mountains.*

   i. They are enjoying the beauty of nature. (........).
   ii. They are planning to climb up to the highest peak of the mountain. (........).
   iii. They are studying the herbs available on the mountain. (........).
   iv. They have become tired after a lot of walking and are just relaxing. (........).
   v. They are thinking about the new techniques of mountaineering. (........).
   vi. They are thinking of writing a report after having inspected the mountainous region. (........).

4. *A farmer's son is ploughing the field.*

   i. He is contributing his share to make up the deficit of food in the country. (........).

   ii. He is thinking of sowing after he has ploughed the land. (........) .

  iii. He is trying to get the maximum possible yield from his land. (........).

  iv. He is ploughing the land to get sufficient food for himself and his family. (........).

   v. He is ploughing the field to sow seeds. (........).

  vi. He is using chemical fertilizers to make the land more productive. (........)

5. *A boy is doing something in the laboratory.*

   i. He is thinking that he should discover some new thing. (........)

  ii. He is practicing an experiment for the examination. (........)

 iii. He is clearing the instruments kept in the laboratory. (........)

 iv. He is busy in discovering new things. (........)

  v. He is doing an experiment in science. (........)

 vi. He is looking at instruments placed in the laboratory. (........).

7. *A man and a boy are sitting with a tabla.*

   i. The boy is learning to play on the tabla. (........)

  ii. The boy is learning the tricks of the trade from his teacher in order to become a good musician. (........)

 iii. They are wondering as to why other persons have not turned up so far. (........)

 iv. The boy is preparing for the examination in music. (........)

  v. The boy is absorbed in learning new music compositions form that man. (........)

 vi. They are playing on the tabla to entertain themselves. (........).

8. *Two boys are playing hockey.*

   i. They are playing hockey to pass the evening. (........)

  ii. They are learning hockey from the instructor. (........)

 iii. They are practicing hockey to regain the trophy lost by them in the last competition. (........)

 iv. They are playing for their amusement. (........)

  v. They are playing hockey to check whether the ground is suitable for playing a hockey match. (........)

vi.   They are preparing the final hockey match. (........).

9. ***A teacher and some boys are in the class.***

i.   They are participating in a discussion competition on 'How to check the growing indiscipline in schools'. (........)

ii.   They are learning a new lesion from the teacher. (........)

iii.   They are getting a complicated problem solved by the teacher. (........)

iv.   They are taking part in a group discussion to evolve indigenous methods to solve the food problem. (........)

v.   They are talking with the teacher. (........)

vi.   They are learning a new formula in mathematics from their teacher. (........).

10. ***A teacher is sitting in a chair. A boy is standing by his side.***

i.   The boy is informing the teacher about the truants. (........)

ii.   That boy has now developed a new thing and he is eager to show it to the teacher. (........)

iii.   The boy is standing beside the teacher to recite his lesson. (........)

iv.   The boy is standing there to hand over a letter from his father to the teacher. (........)

v.   He is standing there to show the teacher the essay that he has prepared to submit for the essay competition. (........)

vi.   He is standing there to understand a problem from his teacher. (........)

11. ***A boy is reading something.***

i.   He is looking for the meaning of that word nobody could tell in the class. (........)

ii.   He is reading a book of stories to pass the time. (........)

iii.   He is reading about new discoveries made in the different fields. (........)

iv.   He is preparing the lesson assigned to him by his teacher. (........)

v.   He is enjoying a book of film songs. (........)

vi.   He is preparing for some competitive examination. (........)

12. ***The principal is giving something to a boy.***

   i. He is presenting a certificate to that boy for keeping up the name of the school in the last competition. (........)

  ii. He is praising that boy for maintaining discipline in the class. (........)

 iii. He is giving some important instructions to that boy. (........)

 iv. He is giving a prize to the boy for his courageous act. (........)

  v. He is giving a booklet of rules and regulations to the boy for forthcoming regional competition. (........)

 vi. He is giving the attendance register to the boy for taking attendance of the class in the absence of the class teacher. (........)

13.   ***Some boys are playing cricket.***

   i. They are learning to play cricket. (........)

  ii. They are trying to improve their game. (........)

 iii. They are playing to pass their recess. (........)

 iv. They are practicing the game. (........)

  v. They are preparing to take party in the annual school competition. (........)

 vi. They are playing an exhibition match to collect funds. (........)

14.   ***A boy is holding some arrows in his hand. There is a target board placed at some distance.***

   i. That boy is waiting for the end of the P.T. period, so that he can go home. (........)

  ii. He is learning the art of arrow-shooting. (........)

 iii. He is practicing arrow-shooting to become a good arrow-shooter. (........)

 iv. He is trying to finish this game quickly so that he can play some other game. (........)

  v. He is thinking of different techniques of shooting. (........)

 vi. He is practicing in order to get the first position in the arrow-shooting competition. (........)

15.   ***A doctor is sitting with a patient.***

   i. He is talking to the patient. (........)

  ii. He is carefully examining the patient. (........)

 iii. The doctor has given an injection to the patient and now he is waiting for his fee. (........)

iv. The doctor is prescribing the diet for him. (........)

v. The doctor is carefully listening to the patient so that he can diagnose his disease properly. (........)

vi. The doctor is giving an injection to the patient to make him healthy. (........)

16. *A boy is sitting under a lamp. He has a book in his hand.*

i. He is thinking of doing some great work after completing his studies. (........)

ii. He is thinking that now he should start preparing for the examination. (........)

iii. He is trying to write something in the book. (........)

iv. He is preparing all the possible questions which can be asked in the examination, so that he may score the highest marks in the class. (........)

v. He is turning the pages of the book and trying to find out that page on which the questions to be asked by the teacher on the following day is given. (........)

vi. He is checking whether there is any name written on the book that he found on way back from school. (........)

17. *A boy is doing something with the help of a hammer and a chisel.*

i. He is making a model. (........)

ii. He is trying to improve his skill in the craft. (........)

iii. He is checking whether the hammer and chisel work properly. (........)

iv. He is repairing the broken model. (........)

v. He is trying to become a sculptor. (........)

vi. By doing this he is getting physical exercise. (........).

18. *A boy is standing with a pen in his hand. He has a notebook.*

i. He will fill in the ink and write something on the note-book. (........)

ii. He is thinking of writing an interesting story. (........)

iii. He is imagining that he will become a writer. (........)

iv. He is checking whether the pen writes properly. (........)

v. He is thinking of the outlines for an essay for a competition. (........)

vi. He is solving assigned questions on the note-book with the help of that pen. (........)

9. *Some persons are doing various types of work.*

i. They are discussing as to what they would do so that they can progress. (........)
ii. They are busy in their respective tasks. (........)
iii. They are working to earn money. (........)
iv. They are thinking about various ways to march ahead on the path of progress. (........)
v. They are doing their work. (........)
vi. A man has to do something to earn his livelihood. These people are also doing some such work. (........)

20. *A boy is flying a kite.*

i. He is amusing himself. (........)
ii. He is thinking as to how he should fly the kite so that he may win the kite-flying competition. (........)
iii. He is wondering whether he should participate in the kite-flying competition on the following day. (........)
iv. He has just bought the kite out of the money that he got from his mother and is now trying to fly it. (........)
v. He is thinking of becoming a good kite-flier so that he may compete with his companions. (........)
vi. He is thinking whether he should compete with the other kite-flier. (........).

21. *The teacher is teaching in the class.*

i. The teacher is trying to complete the course. (........)
ii. He is teaching to earn his salary. (........)
iii. He is making a study of the effective methods of teaching. (........)
iv. He is answering the questions put to him by the students. (........)
v. He is punishing those students who have not done their work. (........)
vi. He is making a difficult lesson easier by giving new examples. (........)

22. *Three boys are running a relay race.*

i. They are practicing in order to improve their performance. (........)
ii. They are learning the relay race during the games period. (........)
iii. They are carrying out instructions. (........)
iv. They are trying to surpass each other in the race. (........).
v. They are demonstrating their skill. (................).
vi. They are observing sports day. (....................).

<u>Appendix-II</u>

Socio economic status scale of Nayak (2005)

SES scale of Nayak (*weightage of items appear in parenthesis*)

A: Personal background data

(i) Name

(ii) Name of your father

(iii) Name of your mother

(iv) Number of person in your family

(v) Nature of family – nuclear/ Joint.

(vi) Age

(vii) Caste

(viii) Gender

B: Education

Educational qualification of your father / mother

IAS/ CA/ MBA/ CS: [10]

SAS/ Engineer/ Medical: [09]

MA/ M Sc/ M Com/ LLM: [08]

BA/ B Sc/ B Com/ LLB: [07]

IA/ I Sc/ I Com: [06]

H SCE/ H SC: [05]

Middle school level: [04]

Primary level: [03]

Illiterate: [02]

C: Occupation

Indicate what the occupation of your father / mother is

Administrative Service: [10]

Company services: [09]

Engineer/ Doctor: [08]

College Teachers: [06]

Clerical: [06]

Workers: [05]

Skilled: [04]
Non-skilled: [03]
Unemployed: [02]
D: Income
Above Rs. 50,000: [10]
Rs. 40,000 to Rs. 49,999: [09]
Rs. 30,000 to Rs. 39,999: [08]
Rs. 20,000 to Rs. 29,999: [07]
Rs. 10,000 to Rs. 19,999: [06]
Rs. 1,000 to Rs. 9,999: [05]
Below Rs. 1,000: [04]
Material wealth: [03]
Building: [02]

Total Score	SES
16 – 29	High
> 16	Low

www.ingramcontent.com/pod-product-compliance
Lightning Source LLC
Chambersburg PA
CBHW051356150726
48000CB00003B/1217